The Streetsweeper

Written by Sharon Parsons

Illustrated by Rae Dale

Contents	Page
Chapter 1. *A smelly morning*	4
Chapter 2. *Grouchy moods*	9
Chapter 3. *Too many important people*	15
Chapter 4. *Streetsweeper strike!*	18
Chapter 5. *A flood*	25
Verse	32

The Streetsweeper

With these characters ...

Joe Delaney

Dr. Maldon

Silvio DiMario

Sarah Seltzer

"I've just stepped in something

Setting the scene ...

Three people who think their jobs are very important live on Wattle Street. When Joe Delaney tries to sweep their street, all they do is complain. Joe decides to show them just why his job is important, too! Very soon, Wattle Street starts to look *very* different!

smelly and it's your fault!"

Chapter 1.

"Pooh!" said Dr. Maldon. "What is that smell?" She looked at the seat beside her. There was nothing smelly there. She looked over her shoulder. There was only her sweater on the back seat. She sniffed again. All she could smell was her perfume, called "Sensational." At least it was not *her* that smelled terrible.

"Ahhh!"

Dr. Maldon took a deep breath of the morning air. The wattle trees on Wattle Street smelled like honey. She slammed the door of her sports car, ready to drive to the hospital. Then Dr. Maldon wrinkled her nose and sniffed. Something in the car smelled terrible!

Finally, she looked down at her shoes.

"Oh, yuck! Those disgusting crab apples from the tree next door!" she grumbled. She leaped out of her car and wiped her shoes on the grass. After climbing back in, she fumbled around in her handbag. Bringing out her bottle of perfume, she sprayed it inside the car.

Dr. Maldon sputtered as perfume went up her nose. "That smells better," she thought. She drove down Wattle Street in a cloud of perfume. As she drove around the corner, she slammed on the brakes.

In front of Dr. Maldon was a huge, yellow streetsweeper. Its orange lights were flashing and its brushes were whirring around. It moved along the street, sweeping up the trash.

Dr. Maldon waved at the driver of the streetsweeper.

"Get out of my way, you silly man," she called. "I'm Dr. Maldon and I'm a *very* important doctor. You're blocking the road!"

Chapter 2.

Joe Delaney, the driver of the streetsweeper, pulled over. Dr. Maldon drove her car next to the streetsweeper. She gave him a grumpy look.

"I'm really sorry," said Joe with a surprised look. "I'm only doing my job."

"Well, you're not doing a very good job," she said grumpily. "I just stepped in something smelly and it's your fault!"

Joe sniffed. All he could smell was Dr. Maldon's perfume, wafting out her car window. "Something does smell a bit odd," he agreed.

Dr. Maldon quickly wound up her window. She tried to think of something rude to say to him. When she couldn't think of anything, she rudely tooted her horn and drove off down the road.

"Well, well! Some people are just too important to be polite," said Joe to himself.

Joe Delaney turned the streetsweeper onto Wattle Street. A cloud of dust blew up as the brushes cleaned the gutter. They whizzed and whirred. Joe squeezed the streetsweeper past a car parked in the street.

A man in a dark blue suit and shiny black shoes rushed out from his house. He waved his arms at Joe, and then he pointed at his car. Joe made the brushes slow down and leaned out the window.

"Look at all the dust that's blowing over my car!" shouted the man. "I just washed it and now it's dirty again."

"I'm really sorry," said Joe. "I'm only doing my job."

"My name's Silvio DiMario and I'm a very important lawyer. I could get you into big trouble for this mistake," grumbled the man. He marched back up his sidewalk. His shiny black shoes squeaked with every step.

Joe wondered why the doctor and the lawyer were in such grouchy moods. After all, he was only doing his job, making Wattle Street look cleaner and more beautiful. Perhaps very important people were *too* important to be in a good mood.

Chapter 3.

Joe drove on down Wattle Street.
His streetsweeper rumbled and roared
as it swept along the gutter. Then
he turned the streetsweeper around
to sweep the other side of the street.

Joe noticed a woman standing on the
sidewalk with her hands on her hips.

"Can't you drive that sweeping thing more quietly?" she called out gruffly. "I'm Sarah Seltzer, a very important TV news reporter. I'm trying to write an important story for tonight's news!"

"Three important people on one street," thought Joe to himself. He raised his hands and said, "I'm *really* sorry, I'm only doing my job." After saying that three times, Joe felt like a robot!

Sarah Seltzer stomped back up her sidewalk. She said a few more words that Joe was glad he couldn't hear. She slammed her front door loudly.

That was the last straw! Joe didn't think this was fair. These people thought they were more important than he was. "Hey!" thought Joe. "I know how to show them just how important my job really is!"

Chapter 4.

Joe Delaney parked the streetsweeper and turned off the flashing lights. He switched off the whizzing brushes. Then Joe fumbled around behind his seat. He found a thick marker pen and a large piece of paper. He wrote a sign in capital letters.

When he had finished writing the sign, he stuck it on the windshield. He climbed out of the streetsweeper and walked home, whistling a tune.

When Dr. Maldon drove home that evening, she was surprised to see the streetsweeper. Even more surprising, she saw Silvio DiMario and Sarah Seltzer standing beside it. She noticed Joe's big sign on the windshield. Dr. Maldon stopped and read the sign.

> MY NAME IS JOE DELANEY.
> I'M A VERY IMPORTANT STREETSWEEPER!
>
> P.S. I'M ON STRIKE!

"How long is that ugly sweeper thing going to be parked here?" she asked Silvio and Sarah. "It's an eyesore!"

Silvio DiMario started to speak, but Sarah Seltzer spoke first.

"Who does this Joe Delaney think he is?" complained Sarah. "I should write a report about this shocking streetsweeper driver for tomorrow night's news."

"Doesn't he care who we are?" asked Silvio. "I should get him into big trouble with the law!"

But no one did anything. They just complained to each other. After all, they were *too* important to worry about a streetsweeper driver going on strike. Somebody else should fix the problem!

Every day, Joe Delaney walked to Wattle Street, sat in his streetsweeper, and read the newspaper. At lunchtime, he ate his sandwich and drank his coffee.

During the afternoon, he finished reading his newspaper and walked home at five o'clock.

People had become used to the streetsweeper cleaning up after them. So by the end of the second week of the streetsweeping strike, Wattle Street was littered with trash.

Each morning, Dr. Maldon had to carefully walk around all the dirt. The inside of her sports car smelled like the inside of her "Sensational" perfume bottle.

Lots of trash became snagged underneath Silvio DiMario's car. He didn't even bother cleaning it anymore.

Every time the wind blew, bottles and cans clattered past Sarah Seltzer's house.

By the end of the third week,
Wattle Street looked like a trash dump.
Litter ended up everywhere, because
everyone was too important to clean up.
When it started to rain, Wattle Street
looked like a floating trash dump!

Chapter 5.

The rain washed all the trash into the gutters. Soon there was so much trash, the gutters became blocked. With nowhere to go, the water overflowed and flooded Wattle Street.

Dr. Maldon felt sick when she saw trash floating on her front lawn. She put her raincoat on over her nightgown and rushed outside.

Sarah Seltzer was already outside, wearing rubber boots and a raincoat. Silvio DiMario squished along the path wearing slippers and striped pajamas.

They stared at each other and then at the streetsweeper. Inside the cab, safe from the rain, Joe sipped a cup of coffee.

Dr. Maldon sloshed up to the streetsweeper and tapped on the window. Joe wound down the window and smiled.

"Good morning, Dr. Maldon. Don't you have something more important to do?" he asked.

Dr. Maldon looked embarrassed. Silvio DiMario and Sarah Seltzer sploshed up to the streetsweeper, too.

"Ah," said Joe, finishing his cup of coffee. "Two *more* important people with nothing better to do. How can I help you all?"

By now, all three were dripping with water. They were drenched.

"We're very sorry, Mr. Delaney. We were rude to you, and you were only doing your job," said Silvio, sputtering and shivering.

"We've learned our lesson," added Sarah Seltzer. She pulled her soaking, wet hair away from her eyes.

"Could you *please* stop your strike, Mr. Delaney?" asked Dr. Maldon politely. "Wattle Street will turn into a river! We need your help now."

Joe pretended to think very hard. Then he smiled.

"Well, I am the only person here who knows how to sweep streets. So, I suppose that means I *am* important," he said. "Far too important to be talking on the job."

He reached forward and switched the streetsweeper's engine on. A huge spray of water flew up as the brushes spun around.

Smelly puddle water sprayed over Dr. Maldon's boots. The sound of cans and bottles rattled in Sarah's ears. Mud and trash splashed onto Silvio's car. Everyone became even more drenched.

Joe and his streetsweeper had started to clean up the trash dump on Wattle Street. But no one complained. After all, Joe was only doing his job!